108 Meditations on Silence

108 Meditations on Silence

Stuart Rose

Diggory Press

British Library Cataloguing In
Publication Data
A Record of this Publication is available
from the British Library

ISBN 1846851688
978-1-84685-168-1

First Published April 2006 by

Exposure Publishing,
an imprint of Diggory Press,
Three Rivers, Minions, Liskeard,
Cornwall, PL14 5LE, UK
WWW.DIGGORYPRESS.COM

Silence is the ocean in which all the rivers of all the religions discharge themselves.

Thayumanavar

If there is no silence beyond and within the many words of doctrine, there is no religion, only a religious ideology. For religion goes beyond words and actions, and attains the ultimate truth only in silence and Love.

Thomas Merton

Preface

The first level or starting point of silence is the cessation of speech. Once this has been maintained for a short while, we can notice that our speech continues in the form of thought. In fact, speech and thoughts may be considered as one and the same: speech being the external projection, albeit with control and selection, of thought, which in contrast is wholly internal.

The silence with which these meditations is concerned is to do with the spiritual practice of controlling, quietening, and – in its complete sense – the silencing of all thought.

In all spiritual practice and in all religions, effort is made to quieten and silence the mind in order to bring oneself closer to God. The word 'God' is used here to signify that highest element, the ultimate truth, of all spiritual paths. It therefore also encompasses Adonai, Allah, Brahman, Buddahood, Absolute Reality, and all such words.

If God can be thought to have characteristics, prime among these will be silence. In our spiritual practice, by quietening ourselves, making our minds silent, we bring ourselves as close as it is humanly possible to God. According to belief, on the one hand this allows God to enter more deeply into the individual, on the other hand for the individual to become merged with God.

In these meditations there is no conflict of belief. Whether God is seen to be wholly separate from the individual and a personal God, or whether God and the individual are, in absolute terms, seen to be one and the same, makes no difference. The prime objective of all spiritual paths, through practice, is to bring ourselves to that high point where communion with God can be at its very closest, its most refined.

Some people may not be able to find such a silence through meditation, and use other means to achieve the same end, for example, through prayer, chanting or singing, repetition of certain names or phrases, and so forth. There are many ways to God. However, in the end, we come to a point, brief though it may be for some, of an inner and deep quietness, as if there is a current or sea running underneath the waves of these activities, so to speak, which we identify as being closest to God.

This is not a belief, but a knowledge born out of real experience. It cannot be conveyed with any accuracy to another person, but nevertheless is real beyond any question. With continued practise, this experience can be deepened, broadened, and made more expansive, while, at the same time, attachments to the world naturally may fall away as the closeness or merging is made more complete.

This closeness does not call for a renunciation of the world; life's normal activities can continue. This is because the closeness is wholly self-contained. Its outer 'showings' may be in the form of a greater honesty, being wiser, more loving, gentler, quieter, more temperate, and so forth, although these may not 'show' at all. Yet they will exist.

Silence is made deeper and stronger when there is peace. Whether the world is at peace or not is of no concern. This peace is an internal tranquillity, where our thoughts are undisturbed or not distracted, or less so, by whatever is happening to us or around us. With such an aide, this deep inner silence can become strong beyond belief.

The number 108 is auspicious, although its origin is lost in the mist of time. Perhaps it is based on the number three which, in many religions, holds an important place: as in the Three Jewels of Buddhism, and the Christian and Hindu trinities.

These meditations can be read singly or collectively. Each, with contemplation, can lead the reader into deeper levels of thought about what silence is, and what part it can play in the spiritual practice.

The word 'silence' is equivalent to the word 'God' in its inference. In these meditations, the two words are often used interchangeably. True silence holds such a place.

Stuart Rose
Camlad House, Wales
stuart.rose@britishlibrary.net

March 2006

The Meditations

1

There is no Silence;

There is only Silence.

When I listen,

I hear;

When I listen,

There is nothing to hear.

2

There is a quietness in my soul,
In amongst the hubbub,
Or so it seems;
But clear away the hubbub
And there's nothing there.

3

To those who know stillness
Nothing ever happens,
But forgetfulness muddies the water
And all hell breaks loose.

4

I can be quiet now.
Will I be quiet then.

Your Silence is my Silence.

Your breath is my breath.

One Silence, one breath.

One.

6

No matter how much noise
and movement.
Always Silence.
Always stillness.
Never more. Never less.
Always.

You speak no words,

Beloved Master,

Yet I hear You clearly.

When I listen.

8

Speak to me.
And You do.
In Silence.

9

The more I am quiet,

The more You hear me.

Beloved One.

You have no stealth,

You are everywhere.

You surprise me,

When I do not listen.

10

There is no Silence in the future,

Nor in the past.

Silence is now.

Thoughts of past and future

Are only the babble of the mind.

11

Every sound is You calling.
Waking me up,
To the Silence.

Every sound is You calling.
I should listen intently,
To everything You have to say,
Feeding on every note.
Never satiated.

Every sound is You calling.
Each is the sound of love.
It cannot be heard,
Except by those with open arms.

12

Even though I cannot see You,
You fill me with your Silence,
Which is love.
I am always brimming full.
You always add more.
You have no limit.

There is nothing more to You
than Silence.
I bring You my heart,
It is everything I can give.

14

What is real cannot be spoken of,
Or thought of.
It is found in Silence alone.

This Silence is not a flat land,
Its depth is unfathomable in all directions.

Love is the key to unlock
the unlocked Silence,
To where I can swim forever.

The silent song wells up in my heart
Filling my entirety.
There is no limit to the song:
All pitches, all notes, all voices.
It is the song that cannot be heard
But which drowns out all else;
It is the song I sing with You,
O Beloved,
Throughout my whole being.
I cannot sing this song enough,
It fills me with love for You,
O bounteous One.

There is no Silence in the world.
There is no Silence in the mind.
Everywhere I look
Silence cannot be found.
But when I look at You,
Beloved One,
There is Silence everywhere.

Where am I going to find Silence

in this place,

Or that.

Where peace.

Where happiness.

Who is it who wants to be silent.

Not me, said the mind,

Who enjoys distractions.

I want to find Silence.

Who is it that seeks.

Silence is not to be found.

No amount of pleading

Will reap the reward of Silence.

Sit and wait.

Do nothing.

I cannot find Silence

No matter where I look.

Do away with the I,

And looking stops in Silence.

22

Love unconditionally.
There, Silence reigns.

The gateway to Silence
Needs a key.
Once the key is found,
Where is the gate.

Exquisite, beautiful, wondrous,

Is Silence.

What can be said of that which is not

Silence.

O Silence,

You are all things everywhere.

Beloved Silence.

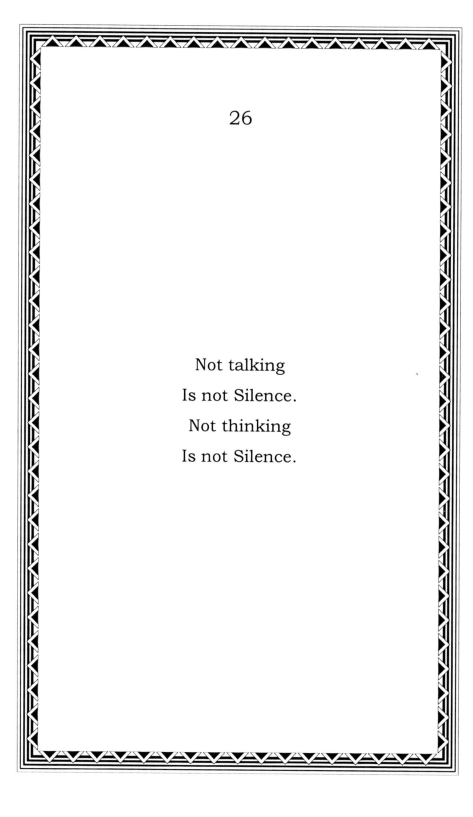

26

Not talking
Is not Silence.
Not thinking
Is not Silence.

Love Silence.

Feed off Silence:

The most nourishing and tasty

Of all foods.

28

How small shall the ego be
To reveal the fullness of Silence.
The size of a pea,
A pin head.
Size does not matter.
Silence is all sizes.

29

The louder the Silence
The lower the voice.

Silence is

When all doors fly open,

When all barriers come down.

Nothing intervenes.

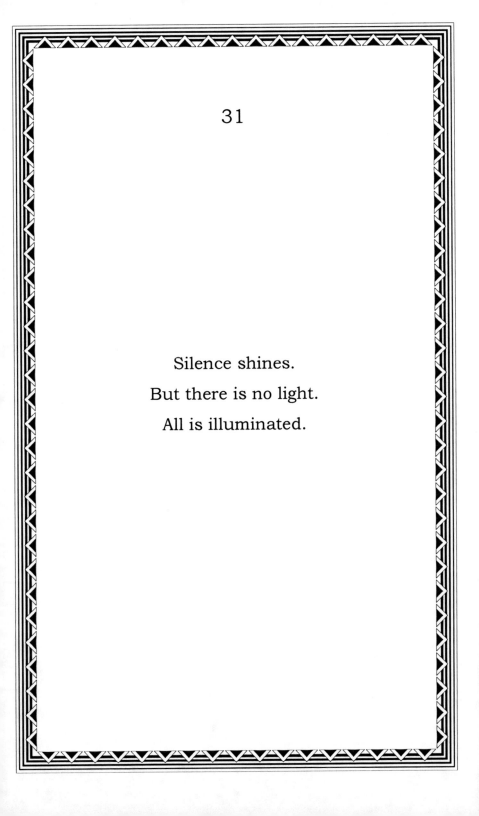

31

Silence shines.
But there is no light.
All is illuminated.

32

The louder the ego
The quieter is Silence.
The quieter the ego,
The more deafening is Silence.

Silence is not about sound,

It is about ego.

Turn the volume of the ego right down,

And all will be revealed.

34

Silence almost comes,
Then at the last moment
It slithers away into a new thought.
O Silence, You cannot be caught;
But when I sit quietly,
Here You are.
You are here all of the time
To be enjoyed without struggle,
Without effort.

35

Silence this voice.

Then there will only be Silence.

Silence of the ego.

O glorious Silence.

O peacefulness and calm.

O equanimity and clarity.

O quietude and Silence.

O.

Is there anywhere that is Silence.

Is it in the woods, the sea, my cell.

Is it in space, a womb, my mind.

Yes, it is in all these and more.

Silence is everywhere,

But it cannot be heard.

Dispeller of all pain and agony.

O Silence,

You are wondrous indeed.

Words are nonsensical

In comparison

To that which is said in Silence.

41

Silence is not the sound
When the washing machine stops,
Or when lawn mowing finishes,
Or when, at twilight, birds cease calling,
Or the momentary lull after
a wave crashes,
Or a car crashes,
Or a shotgun blast.
Silence never ends,
Never changes.
Forever always in me.

42

There is no hiding from Silence,

Yet it is usually ignored,

And life goes by.

Catch up with Silence anytime.

43

Above, around, behind, and all through
The cackle of the mind,
Silence can be heard.
It can be heard right at this moment.

How can I be silent when there is

So much going on

In my mind.

Listen.

Silence is always here.

Never doubt it.

45

Silence comes of its own accord.

Push as hard as possible,

It is of no use.

Silence will not be pushed, cajoled,

or bought.

It is here anyway.

Wait and see.

Glorious Silence.

I love You, Silence.

My heart is full of joy

When You become clear,

And I remain glowing

After You are obscured.

I just have to look

At your beautiful face,

And we are One again.

O beloved Silence.

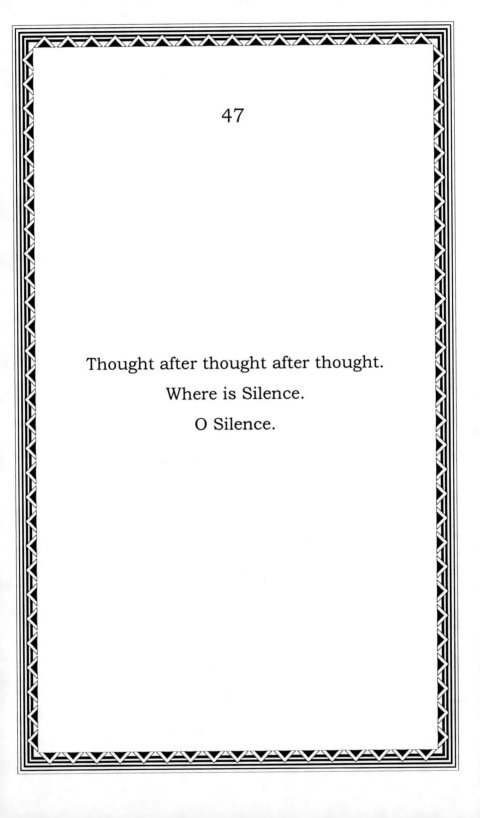

47

Thought after thought after thought.

Where is Silence.

O Silence.

Forget the mind.

Forget me.

Remember Silence.

Beautiful Silence.

Concentrating on Silence,

The path to it

Simply disappears.

The goal is reached.

Silence curls around me,

More penetrating

Than the strongest perfume.

It transfixes me

In the greatest of all happinesses.

O Silence,

Beautiful Silence.

Though this mind keeps moving,

Chattering and chuntering,

It does not matter.

This mind cannot influence,

Or even interrupt,

The flow of Silence.

Wondrous Silence.

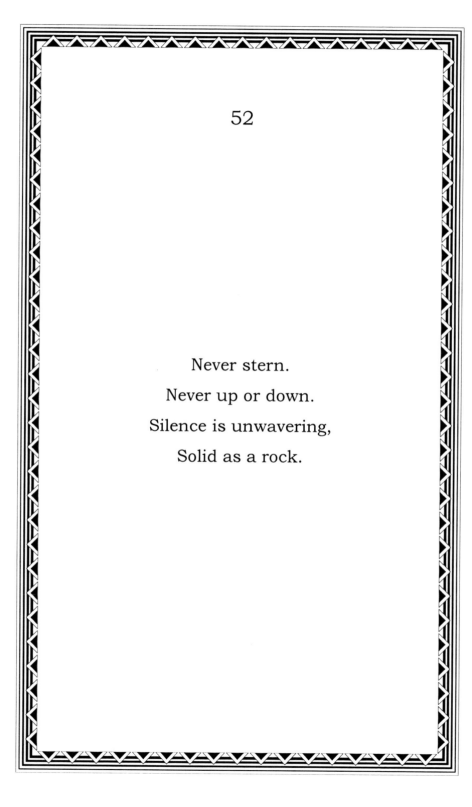

Never stern.

Never up or down.

Silence is unwavering,

Solid as a rock.

Do not look for Silence in the world,

It cannot be found.

And the same can be said of the mind.

Look otherwise for Silence,

Where it is plain to see.

54

Silence is here,
Silence is there.
Do not be mistaken,
Silence is everywhere.

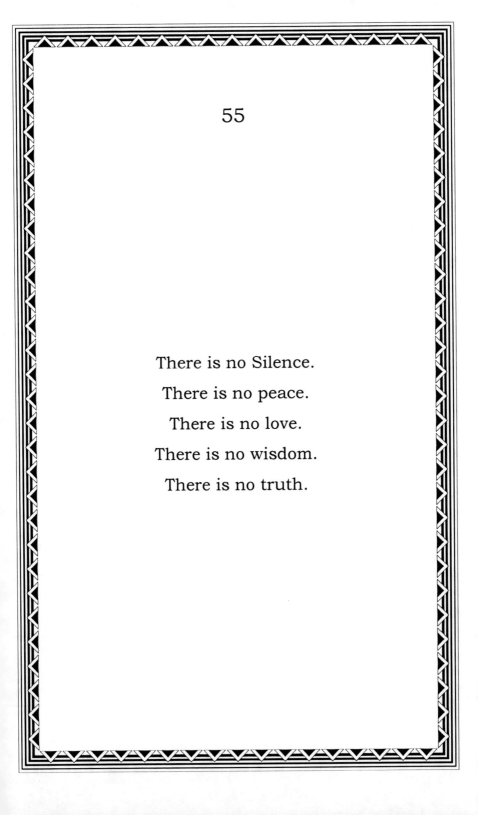

55

There is no Silence.

There is no peace.

There is no love.

There is no wisdom.

There is no truth.

Silence is only found in one place.

Seek as far as I may,

Always only one place.

Beloved love.

You lay the gift of Silence

At my feet.

You spoon feed me

Morsel after morsel

Of this nectar,

And I grow more and more silent

In your watchfulness.

There is only restlessness in the mind,
Disparity and dysfunction,
But in Silence,
Everything falls into place
Of its own accord.
Beloved Silence.

There is Silence
Behind the purr of a cat,
Behind a baby's cry,
Behind laughter,
And the roar of jet engines,
Behind a kiss,
And symphonies and quartets,
Behind quietness,
Behind all.
Yet not just behind,
Silence is throughout.
Inescapable,
Once heard.

Silence exists while having breakfast,

Driving along,

Singing a song,

At the workplace,

Sound asleep.

Silence is everywhere.

What a wonder.

Silence is the end of everything.

Beloved Silence.

This life is of no consequence.

O bounteous One.

Silence is all.

The world is quieter when there is fog,
Yet there is no quiet in a foggy mind.
Silence is crystal clear.
It is where all is known.

63

Silence is all around me,
Far, far beyond me,
And throughout me.
This me is superfluous.
Better to settle in Silence,
And forget me.

Every time I think,

Silence is pushed away

And I cannot hear it

And I cannot bear it.

Except,

When I think of Silence,

You come flooding back.

O Beloved.

All religions involve returning
to the source,
But we have not left the source.
There is nowhere to come from,
or go to.
All is Silence.
Listen to That.

66

O ego, get out of the way

And all will be quiet.

67

In all the many things to do and think
Each and every day,
Silence is not separate.
Silence permeates all activity and thought.
Listen, and it can be heard,
Whatever is being done.

All is Silence,
Everything is included,
Even the mundane.
Beloved Silence.

Silence can still be heard

While the mind is active.

Listen,

And the mind will quieten.

Listen,

And know this truth.

Listen,

And bliss will flow.

Silence, Silence, Silence, Silence.
Silence, Silence, Silence, Silence.
Silence, Silence, Silence, Silence.
Silence, Silence, Silence.

71

The degree to which Silence is desired

Is the degree to which it is enjoyed.

Wanting more

Gains more.

Not wanting Silence,

None will occur.

The noise which most
drowns out Silence
Is the sound of I:
I this, I that, and I the other,
Seemingly always sounding
Like the bell buoy rocked by waves.
Cast I-ness adrift,
And let Silence be heard.

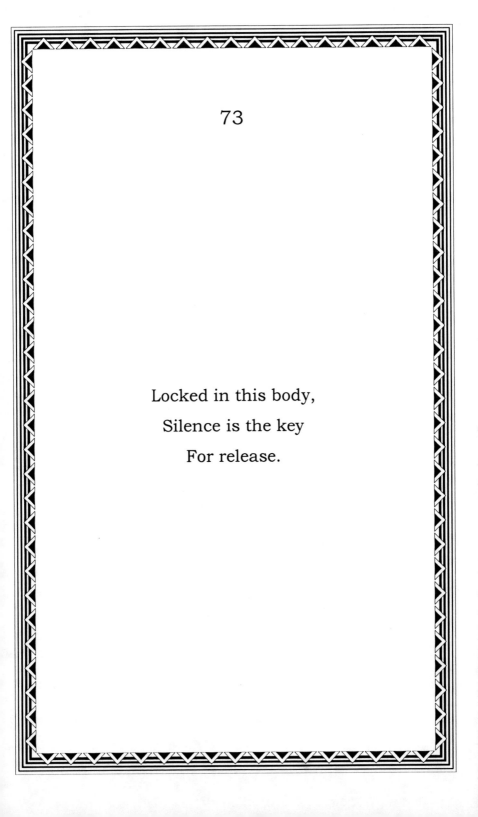

73

Locked in this body,
Silence is the key
For release.

74

O mind, you steal away
the joy of Silence
With your treacherous ways.
You snatch it with distraction,
And fill me with
thoughts of no concern,
Of no value.
Then you catch your breath,
And think thoughts of Silence
once more
(Like clouds passing away
from the sun),
Allowing the bliss of Silence
to shine again.

75

In every kind of sadness,
No matter what depth
Or how much crying,
Even the greatest despair,
Silence is here.
Always unchanging,
Never sad, nor happy,
Never unavailable.
Beloved Silence,
Remover of all sadnesses,
I turn to You.

76

Where does Silence go when I am happy,
Or when I am sad, or worrying,
When I am doing things,
Or when I am with other people.
The legion of times You disappear.

O Silence,
So easily the mind obscures You,
And I lose your beauty,
And I lose your council.

You are always here,
O Beloved.
To see You
All I need to do is think of You.

Who do I think I am
Who thinks I have decided
To sit in Silence.
Beloved Silence,
There are no such decisions.
Just unending You.

My being alive

Does not disturb Silence

In the slightest.

Even when I am dead,

Silence is unperturbed.

Silence is a gift.

It raises me up from the mundane

To where there is no height.

Thoughts are dangerous,
They lead me astray.
Only thoughts of Silence
Bring me home again.

Silence is found in doing good.
Much easier to find
Than in doing the reverse.

Silence is found in peace,
Not in upheaval.

Silence is found in contentment,
Not in commotion.

Silence is found in the heart,
Not outside.

Blessed Silence.

Silence is easy.

It is constant and unchanging,

And not involved in the world.

Silence is always here.

Only Silence.

God is the Silence of me.

84

Noise is ephemeral.

The moon shines in Silence.

The Earth turns in Silence.

The I is silent.

There is not a word that can explain.

No thoughts are my thoughts.

This Silence is not my Silence.

There is the body and the mind.

There is Silence.

Without Silence
There is only anguish.
No joy.
But Silence is only obscured
by the anguish.
Lift the veil,
and the sun will shine.

Slowly thoughts dry up.

Slowly Silence is revealed.

88

O Silence.
Why are you so illusive.
I know you are here,
But I cannot see you
Through this disordered mind.

O Silence.
Foolish me
Who does not remember
That it is this me which is the illusion,
The me that thinks it is the thinker.

O Silence.
That which I am.
That which dissolves the pain of thought,
Yet which has no actions.
Forever serene and unmoving.

O mind,

You can create as much disturbance

As you like

To obscure reality,

But never fear,

Silence always prevails.

There is no end.

Everything ends in tears.

Silence does not end.

No tears.

Silence cannot be silent.

It can always be heard.

Buddhist Silence
Is the same as Christian Silence,
Is the same as Hindu Silence,
Is the same as Islamic Silence,
Is the same as Jewish Silence,
Is the same in every religion.

Lost for words.

Lost in the Silence of God.

Lost everything.

Lost me.

O, the happiness of Silence.

94

The pool of thoughts is murky.

Put all thoughts down,

And there,

In the Silence,

Is clarity.

My mind is weak and feeble,

Filled with constant meaninglessness,

tedious chatter.

O beloved Silence,

Fill me with Your wonder,

And make this mind silent.

I am a fool

If I think I can Silence this mind.

This mind is God's mind,

And it will be Silenced

When God decides.

I am a fool

To think this petty person

Can do anything at all

Without this help.

This mind detests Silence.

It does everything it can

To avoid it.

O Silence,

How can I get the mind

To want You.

O mind,

How can I get you

To want Silence.

Who is this piggy I in the middle.

The mind plays games.

It ducks and weaves,

And will not be caught.

O Silence,

This mind is wily,

It knows the game well

And does not want to lose.

O Silence,

Help me catch this wriggling mind,

And end its game.

Let me rest in Your peace.

O Silence.

This I obscures You.

It holds a curtain of distraction

Over your tranquillity,

And then says I cannot see you.

I am a fool.

Silence the I,

The curtain will fall,

And Silence will be seen.

100

Be at peace,

And Silence will come.

The body quietened

Is where peace will flourish.

The mind at peace

Is where Silence will expand.

The expanse of Silence is measureless.

Bounteous God.

101

More Silence,

More and more and more,

Wider,

Higher,

Deeper,

More and more and more.

102

If Silence feels a long way off
Do not lose heart.
Just remember,
Silence is right behind this thought,
Which is the most flimsy of veils.

Sitting in Silence
Is overwhelming.
I am overwhelmed,
And am no more.

Silence comes in a quiet surge,
Which is a deluge,
And I am obliterated.
Wonderful Silence,
Let it come.

104

Silence in the morning,
Silence in the daytime,
Silence in the evening,
Silence at night.
Silence in the city,
Silence in the country.
Wherever this mind is,
Silence is.

105

Filling my life with sounds
Is not helpful.
It distracts me
From the Silence,
Which remains throughout the sounds,
Unperturbed.
Sounds disturb me,
They lead me away
From the wonderful clarity of Silence.

106

Idle chattering in the mind:

What use is it,

What good is it.

Better to be silent,

And see what that brings.

O Silence.

O sweet Silence,

Wherein no ripples occur,

Where tranquillity has no depth,

Where this I rests in slumber,

Where life is just a passing dream.

O Silence,

I seek to find You, more and more.

You are my one desire,

The one passion.

All that is required

To calm life's storm.

O beloved Silence,

I love You.

I love You, Silence.
I love your calm,
Your peacefulness,
Your quietude.

I love You, Silence.
I love the absence of thoughts,
The absence of I-ness,
The fullness of You.

I love You, Silence.
You are the greatest happiness,
Which is not You or I,
But wondrous, blissful Oneness.

Thank You

To Anna Rose Søvik for the cover art, and the use of the family garden where this book started; to Citisakti and Alan Adams-Jacobs; and to you, the reader, for wanting to discover more about this wonderful subject of silence.

Printed in the United States
87982LV00002B/6/A